THE USBORNE
ANCIENT EGYPT
PICTURE BOOK

ROB LLOYD JONES
ILLUSTRATED BY TONY KERINS

DESIGNED BY SAMANTHA BARRETT
EDITED BY JANE CHISHOLM
EXPERT ADVICE: DR. ANNE MILLARD

CONTENTS

THE LAND OF EGYPT

Around 5,000 years ago, the banks of the Nile were lined with royal palaces, soaring stone pyramids, and beautifully decorated temples and tombs. Here are some of Egypt's most famous sights...

HELIOPOLIS

This ancient town's name means 'city of the sun' in Greek. There was a huge temple here dedicated to Ra, the sun god. Towering stone columns, called obelisks, pointed to the heavens.

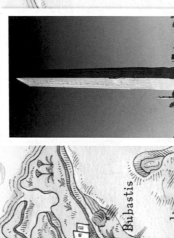
Obelisk from Heliopolis

King Akhenaten

AMARNA

King Akhenaten built Amarna as his capital, in around 1350 BC. Many people hated him because of religious changes he made. So, when he died, the city was destroyed.

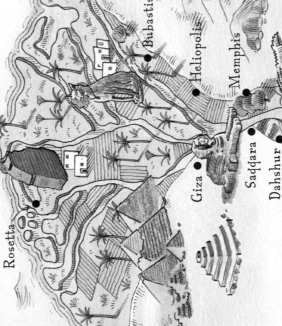

Rosetta

Bubastis

Heliopolis

Memphis

Giza

Saqqara

Dahshur

Amarna

MEMPHIS

Memphis was the capital of Egypt for around 500 years, and one of the biggest cities in the ancient world. Its royal palace was decorated with huge statues of Egyptian kings.

Royal statue from Memphis

N

W — E

Ram statues at Karnak

KARNAK TEMPLE

Karnak, in Thebes, is the biggest temple ever built. It's really lots of temples together, including the Great Temple of Amun. Different Egyptian kings added new parts to show off their power.

Temple ruins on Philae

PHILAE

Philae was a sacred island in the River Nile, with a temple dedicated to the goddess Isis. In the 1800s, tourists visiting Philae nicknamed the island 'The Pearl of the Nile.'

Thebes

Valley of the Kings

Abydos

Edfu

Philae

Abu Simbel

Temple of Horus at Edfu

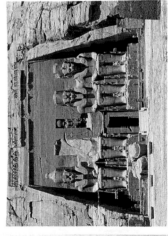
Temple at Abu Simbel

LUXOR TEMPLE

Luxor Temple was dedicated to a powerful god called Amun. The temple was built in the city of Thebes, now called Luxor.

Remains of Luxor Temple

EDFU

The hawk-god Horus was worshipped at this temple in the town of Edfu. The temple was built when Egypt was ruled by Greek kings, called the Ptolemies.

ABU SIMBEL

This magnificent temple was built at Abu Simbel by King Ramesses II. In the 1960s, a project to build a reservoir threatened to flood the site. So, the whole temple was cut from the rock and rebuilt on higher ground.

MIGHTY KINGS

The king, or pharaoh, was at the heart of all life in Egypt. He owned the whole country, led the army, and was worshipped as a god. Here are some of the most famous kings...

MENES

Ruled: from c. 3100BC

Around 5,000 years ago, Egypt was divided into two kingdoms: Upper Egypt (the south) and Lower Egypt (the north). Then, around 3100BC, a ruler called Menes united these two lands. He became the first king of all Egypt.

Kings of Upper Egypt wore the White Crown, and kings of Lower Egypt wore the Red Crown. After Menes united the lands, kings wore the two crowns combined.

MENTUHOTEP II

Ruled: c.2040-2010BC

Mentuhotep II reunited Egypt after a chaotic period of civil war. He also built a magnificent temple on the west bank of the Nile, opposite the city of Thebes.

Sandstone statue of Mentuhotep II

HATSHEPSUT

Ruled: c.1490-1468BC

Hatshepsut was different from most other Egyptian kings – she was a woman. She ruled for 20 years and had several monuments built, including a stunning mortuary temple (for her funeral) cut into the cliffs near Thebes.

Hatshepsut encouraged trade with other countries. Egyptian traders brought luxuries such as incense and ivory back from overseas.

TUTHMOSIS III

Ruled: c.1468-1436BC

During his 30-year reign, Tuthmosis led 17 military campaigns against countries to the north and south of Egypt. Previous kings had also conquered lands overseas, but, under Tuthmosis, Egypt's empire grew larger than ever before.

Some Egyptian kings led their army into battle, riding in golden chariots.

AKHENATEN

Ruled: c1364-1347BC

Egyptians believed in many gods, but Akhenaten introduced a huge religious change, declaring there was just one god, the Aten. Akhenaten was also represented unlike other kings in art – with a long face and curvy body.

Akhenaten and his queen, Nefertiti, threw rewards to officials who gathered outside his palace.

Painted wooden bust of Tutankhamun found in the King's tomb

TUTANKHAMUN

Ruled: c.1347-1337BC

Tutankhamun didn't achieve much in his short reign. But he's very well-known because, around 3,000 years after he died, his tomb became the only royal burial site to be discovered full of golden treasure (see pages 16-17).

RAMESSES II

Ruled: c.1289-1224BC

Almost everything Ramesses II did, he did on a bigger scale than other kings. He ruled for longer (67 years), had more children (around 150), and built more temples, monuments and statues. Today he's known as Ramesses the Great.

Ramesses kept a pet lion, which charged with him into battles.

One story says that Cleopatra deliberately killed herself with a poisonous snake.

CLEOPATRA VII

Ruled: 51-30BC

Famed for her beauty, Cleopatra was the last ruler of Egypt before it was conquered in 30BC by the Romans. After her forces were defeated at the Battle of Actium, off the coast of Greece, Cleopatra committed suicide rather than face surrender.

GODS & GODDESSES

Egyptians worshipped hundreds of gods and goddesses. Most were associated with an animal, and sometimes shown with that animal's head. Many gods had a cult temple dedicated to them in a particular town.

RA

Role: sun god

Associated animal: bull

Cult temple: Heliopolis

Ra – the sun god who created the universe – was the most powerful of all the gods. Sometimes he was joined with the god Horus, and shown with the head of a falcon.

Each night Ra was thought to sail through the land of the dead, defeating evil forces.

AMUN

Two huge temples were built at Thebes to worship Amun.

Role: king of gods

Associated animals: ram, goose

Cult temple: Thebes

Other name: He who lives in all things

At first, Amun was only popular in the city of Thebes. But, as the rulers of Thebes grew more powerful, the cult of Amun spread through Egypt. Eventually he was identified with Ra, and renamed Amun-Ra.

Ptah was usually shown as a mummy holding a staff.

PTAH

Role: god of creation and craftsmen

Associated animal: bull

Cult temple: Memphis

Other name: The ear which hears

In Memphis, people worshipped Ptah (say 'tah') as the most powerful god. They believed he was an architect and craftsman, who built the whole universe, and brought the first Egyptian king to life.

Evil god Set trapped Osiris in a coffin, and pushed it into the Nile.

Painted wooden statue of Osiris

OSIRIS

Role: Ruler of the Underworld

Other name: Ruler of Eternity

Osiris was a great Egyptian king who was murdered by his brother Set, and became Ruler of the Underworld (the land of the dead). A very powerful god, Osiris was usually shown with a green face.

Ma'at was often shown with wings, and an ostrich feather in her hair.

MA'AT

Role: goddess of truth, order and harmony

Ma'at represented the balance of harmony in the universe. Without her, Egyptians believed the world would fall into chaos – famine, wars and deadly disease.

Sometimes Ma'at was represented as a feather on a weighing scale.

ISIS

Role: goddess of mothers and magic

Cult temple: Philae

Other name: Lady of Magic

Isis was Osiris's wife, and the annual flooding of the Nile was thought to be caused by her tears for her dead husband. But, Isis and other gods magically brought him back to life.

Painting of Isis from the wall of a tomb

THE ATEN

Role: creator of the universe

Cult temple: Amarna

A huge religious change took place when Akhenaten decided there was only one god, the Aten. Sculpture from that time shows the king basking under the rays of the Aten, a dazzling sun-disc in the sky.

When Akhenaten died, statues of him were destroyed. It was forbidden for anyone to mention him ever again.

MORE EGYPTIAN GODS

Egyptians believed that there was a god or goddess
to watch over almost every aspect of daily life.
Here are some more popular Egyptian gods...

BASTET

Role: goddess of joy and warmth

Associated animal: domestic cat

Cult temple: Bubastis

Other name: The Eye of Ra

Each year, thousands of Egyptians
flocked to the temple in Bubastis
to celebrate the Feast of Bastet,
a lavish festival in praise of
this popular cat goddess.

Cats were important
animals in Egypt. They
protected food by chasing
off mice, and frightened
away deadly snakes.

HATHOR

Role: goddess of music, love and pregnant women

Associated animal: cow

Cult temple: Dendera

Other name: Mistress of the West

Hathor was thought to protect women during
childbirth, and to welcome dead Egyptians into
the next life. Sometimes, she was shown as an
elegant lady with the horns of a cow, and
a sun-disc sitting between them.

SEKHMET

Role: goddess of war and healing

Associated animal: lioness

Other names: Mistress of Dread, Lady of Slaughter

This fierce lion-headed goddess protected Egyptian
kings in battle, killing their enemies with arrows
of fire. Hot desert winds were thought to be
Sekhmet's scorching breath.

In one myth, Sekhmet went on a furious
rampage, feasting on humans. Ra tricked her
into stopping, by turning the Nile water into
beer. Sekhmet drank until she collapsed.

Statue of Anubis
found in the tomb
of King Tutankhamun

ANUBIS

Role: god of embalming, and guide in the afterlife

Associated animal: jackal

Cult temple: Lycopolis

Other name: Lord of the Place of Embalming

Egyptians believed that, after they died, Anubis
guided them into the next world. They didn't see death
as a bad thing, so Anubis wasn't meant to be evil.

Anubis was thought to have
invented mummification (turning
dead people into mummies).

THOTH

Role: god of wisdom and science

Associated animals: ibis, baboon

Cult temple: Hermopolis

Other name: Lord of Divine Words

In Hermopolis, people believed the
universe began with Thoth.
He was worshipped throughout
Egypt as the inventor of
writing and science.

TAWERET

Associated animal: hippo

Taweret was a female
hippopotamus with long
hair. Sometimes she is
shown with a sun-disc on
her head, and carrying
Egyptian symbols of life.
Taweret was especially
popular with women.

Usually, Thoth was shown with the head of an
ibis, but he was also represented as a baboon.
Egyptians thought baboons were wise, like Thoth.

Statue of Bes,
with lion skin
over shoulders

BES

Role: protector of homes and children

Bes was thought to guard people's
homes, and his scary face frightened
evil spirits away from children. He
was usually shown naked, except for a
lion skin over his back. No one's quite
sure why Bes looks so different from
other Egyptian gods.

Most families had a small
shrine in their home, where
they worshipped statues of
Bes, and other gods.

MAGIC CHARMS

Most Egyptians carried magical charms, called amulets, to protect them or bring good luck. They placed amulets on dead bodies, too, to help the dead person in the afterlife.

EYE OF HORUS

Power in life: heals the sick

Power in death: defeats enemies

The fight between Horus and his evil uncle Set was a popular Egyptian story. Set gouged out Horus's eye, but the eye magically healed. So, this eye amulet was thought to bring good health and the power to defeat enemies.

Horus (with the head of a falcon) and Set fought for control of Egypt.

FISH AMULET

Power in life: protects from drowning

Egyptian women tied charms like this to a lock of their hair. They thought it would help them swim.

This amulet represents a tilapia fish, which were common in the River Nile.

ANKH

Power in life: vitality and strength

Power in death: rebirth into the afterlife

The 'ankh' is the symbol for life in hieroglyphics (Egyptian writing). There are different ideas about what the sign represents – a sandal strap or a belt-buckle.

Egyptian priests read spells over amulets, to give the charms magical powers.

HEART

Power in death: purifies the heart

Egyptians believed that, after they died, gods weighed their hearts to decide whether or not they got into heaven. Heart amulets were laid on mummies to help their hearts pass this test.

SCARAB

Power in life: brings a long life

Power in death: protects your soul

Scarab beetles pushed dung balls up sand dunes to their burrows. Egyptians thought this symbolized the rising sun, so scarab amulets were believed to have life-giving powers.

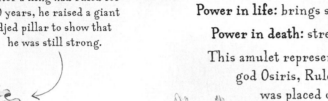

DJED ('JED') PILLAR

Power in life: brings stability and endurance

Power in death: strength in the afterlife

This amulet represented the backbone of the god Osiris, Ruler of the Underworld. It was placed on dead people's necks to help them rise into the afterlife.

After a king had ruled for 30 years, he raised a giant djed pillar to show that he was still strong.

KNOT OF ISIS

Power in life: brings wisdom

Power in death: protects from danger

Most women carried this amulet, which they thought gave them the wisdom of Isis. Some people think it represents the knot the goddess used to hold up her clothes.

MA'AT

Power in life: truth, balance

The winged goddess Ma'at represented the perfect balance of the universe. So, this amulet was supposed to bring order and stability to your life.

Without Ma'at, Egyptians believed the world would fall into chaos – with wars, storms and disease.

ROYAL TOMBS

Early kings built huge pyramid-shaped tombs reaching to the heavens. Later, kings had their tombs cut into cliffs, and decorated inside with scenes of the lives of the gods.

THE STEP PYRAMID

Location: Saqqara

King: Djoser

Completed: 2648BC

King Djoser's Step Pyramid

The first ever pyramid, built for King Djoser, began as a one-layer building. But, so it could be seen better from the desert, another layer was added, and then four more – creating a pyramid.

The Step Pyramid was designed by an architect named Imhotep. Later, Egyptians thought he was so clever that he must have been a god.

THE GREAT PYRAMID

Location: Giza (near Cairo)

King: Khufu

Completed: c.2560BC

The Great Pyramid is the biggest stone structure ever built, made of over 2 million limestone blocks. Each was laid to a careful plan, so the sides were identical in length.

The Great Pyramid

It took around 20,000 workers to build the Great Pyramid. They dragged the stones up a steep ramp to the top.

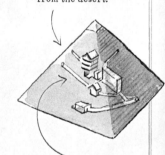

The Great Pyramid rises 147m (482ft) from the desert.

Inside, there are secret passages and rooms. The room in the middle was the King's burial chamber, but no one knows what the others were for.

PYRAMIDS OF KHAFRA AND MENKAURE

Location: Giza

Completed: From 2560 to 2472BC

King Khafra's tomb was built beside the Great Pyramid, and was almost as big. The third pyramid at Giza, for King Menkaure, is smaller – it was finished in a rush after Menkaure died.

The pyramids of Menkaure, Khafra (in the middle) and Khufu

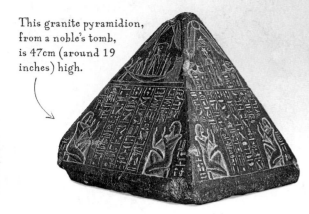

This granite pyramidion, from a noble's tomb, is 47cm (around 19 inches) high.

PYRAMIDION

There was a stone at the very top of a pyramid, called a 'pyramidion'. Usually, it was carved with religious symbols and the name of the person buried inside. Sometimes it was covered in gold, to reflect the dazzling desert sun.

Pyramids were originally encased in white limestone, with a pyramidion at the very top.

THE GREAT SPHINX

Location: Giza

Completed: Around 2560BC

This huge statue was carved from a lump of rock near Khafra's pyramid. With the body of a lion and the head of the King, the Great Sphinx was probably meant to guard the royal tomb.

Some people think the Great Sphinx's nose was blasted off by a soldier's cannon.

The Valley of the Kings

TOMBS IN THE ROCKS

From about 1550BC, Egyptian kings chose to be buried in tombs cut into cliffs near the city of Thebes. They called this royal burial site 'The Great Field', but today it's known as the Valley of the Kings.

Tombs were filled with glittering treasure and decorated with scenes of the gods, and magical spells. The spells were meant to help the kings in the afterlife.

Kings visited their tombs to inspect the work.

Tomb of King Ramesses IV

13

MUMMIES AND COFFINS

Egyptians thought that, after you died, your spirit returned to your body, to eat and drink offerings left in your tomb. So, dead bodies were carefully preserved, or 'mummified', and then laid in beautifully decorated coffins for burial.

ROYAL MUMMIES

Mummification was a very effective way to preserve dead bodies. This mummy, of King Ramesses II, has lasted over 3,200 years. It's shrivelled and dry, but amazingly well preserved.

During the 1800s, it was fashionable to attend 'unwrappings' of mummies brought back to Europe by explorers.

MUMMY MASK

Some mummies had masks over their heads, so the dead person could be recognized in the afterlife. The one on the right belonged to an Egyptian noblewoman, and is decorated with dazzling gold leaf.

MAKING A MUMMY

A dead person's internal organs were placed in 'canopic jars', and left with the body in the tomb. The jars were decorated with the heads of gods thought to protect the body parts.

To make a mummy, the internal organs were taken from the body.

Then, the body was dried in salt for 40 days. Finally, it was wrapped in bandages.

Wooden inner coffins of Egyptian nobles

Once a mummy was ready for burial, priests performed a ceremony to wake the dead person's spirit.

INNER COFFINS

Mummies of wealthy Egyptians were usually placed inside a wooden 'inner coffin'. These caskets were decorated with magical spells that their dead owners needed to survive the dangers of the afterlife.

These two coffins are decorated with spells in hieroglyphics (Egyptian writing), and images of gods and goddesses.

A priest, wearing a mask of a god, lays the mummy in its coffin.

Coffins were decorated on the inside, too.

OUTER COFFINS

If you were really wealthy, you also had two or three 'outer coffins', inside a stone box called a sarcophagus.

Outer coffins were even more beautiful than inner ones, and often covered with real gold.

Outer coffin

Inner coffin

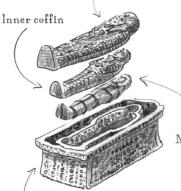

Mummy wearing a mask

Sarcophagus

The faces on these coffins are decorated with gold.

This hefty granite sarcophagus is carved with rectangular 'false doors' through which the owner's spirit was supposed to come and go.

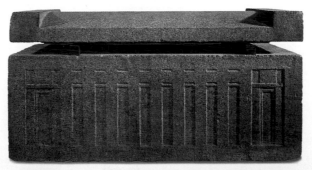

Usually, a sarcophagus was dragged on a sled to the owner's tomb.

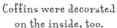

ROYAL TREASURES

From around 3,500 years ago, Egyptian kings were buried in tombs cut into the cliffs of the Valley of the Kings. In 1922, one of these tombs was discovered packed with amazing golden treasure. It belonged to a boy king called Tutankhamun.

WONDERFUL THINGS

The discovery of Tutankhamun's tomb, by British archaeologist Howard Carter, caused a sensation around the world. Everyone was eager to see its treasures, but Carter spent nearly ten years carefully removing each object.

As Carter opened the tomb and peered inside, his friend Lord Carnarvon asked, "Well, do you see anything?" "Yes," Carter replied, "wonderful things..."

Carter had each treasure from the tomb carefully recorded and then wrapped in cloth.

OUTER COFFIN

Tutankhamun's mummy lay inside three coffins, each within the next. This is the second, or intermediate, coffin. It's made of wood covered with gold and precious stones.

DEATH MASK

Tutankhamun's death mask is made of solid gold and precious stones. Placed over the head of the King's mummy, it shows him wearing a royal headdress, with a cobra and vulture – symbols of kingship.

Armed guards kept watch as the priceless treasures were removed from Tutankhamun's tomb.

Tutankhamun's tomb was small compared to others in the Valley of the Kings. This diagram shows the layout.

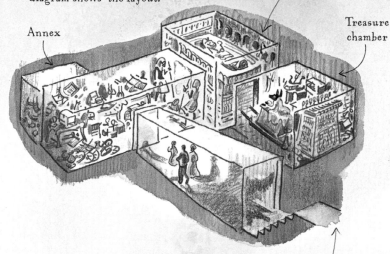

Annex

Burial chamber

Treasure chamber

Entrance to tomb

'KA' STATUE

Two tall wooden statues guarded the entrance to Tutankhamun's burial chamber. They represent the King's spirit (or 'ka'), and were originally wrapped in white linen.

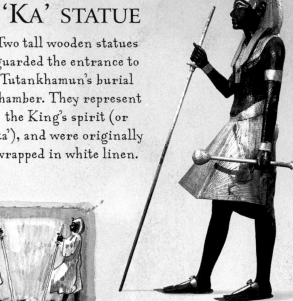

CLOTHES CHEST

This wooden clothes chest was left in the King's tomb, for him to use in the afterlife. It's painted with a scene of Tutankhamun firing arrows as he rides his chariot into battle.

ROYAL THRONE

This royal throne is richly decorated with glimmering gold leaf, ivory and precious stones. The scene on the backrest shows Tutankhamun with his wife, Queen Ankhesenamun.

STORAGE JARS

Ornate jars were left in Tutankhamun's tomb, filled with items the King would need in the afterlife. The one on the left was crammed with glittering jewels, while the alabaster jar on the right held a lotion to keep the King clean.

Unlike Tutankhamun's, all other royal tombs found so far in Egypt were raided by thieves. They burrowed in through the rock and stole all the treasures inside.

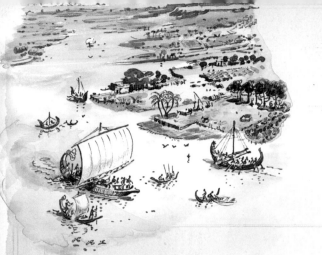

THE MIGHTY NILE

All life in Egypt relied on the River Nile, which provided water to drink and fish to eat, and made the land along its banks lush and fertile to grow crops.

FISHING BOAT

This model from a tomb shows a group of fishermen rowing boats made from papryus reeds. They dragged a net through the water between the boats, and scooped up fish.

Fishermen held competitions to push each other off their boats.

SAILING SHIP

Wooden sailing ships made long journeys to other lands across the Mediterranean Sea. They brought back luxuries to sell in Egypt – cedar wood, copper and oil.

Huge cargo barges carried heavy stones for building works.

Small wooden models like these were often left in tombs. The crew on the ships were meant to serve the tomb owner in the next life.

FUNERAL BARQUE

Brightly painted funeral barques carried dead bodies from the east bank of the Nile (where people lived) to the west (where people were buried).

ANIMALS OF THE NILE

The Nile was home to all kinds of birds and beasts. Egyptians hunted some of them for food. Others they feared, or worshipped as gods.

Lots of birds nested among the marshy banks of the Nile. The heron (left) and geese (right) are paintings from the walls of tombs.

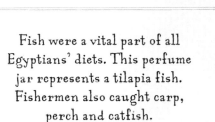

Egyptian nobles hunted birds for sport. They used throw-sticks to hit them in the air.

Fish were a vital part of all Egyptians' diets. This perfume jar represents a tilapia fish. Fishermen also caught carp, perch and catfish.

This fish-shaped jar was meant for holding perfume.

Hippos, which lurked among the Nile's reed thickets, were dangerous beasts. Hunting them was a great way for Egyptian men to show off their courage.

Crocodiles were feared and respected by Egyptians as sacred animals. To keep these creatures from attacking people, Egyptians prayed to a crocodile god called Sobek.

Some crocodiles were kept in lakes at temples, and fed by priests.

EGYPTIAN JOBS

Rich Egyptians had an easy life. But everyone else worked, and worked hard. Here are some of the jobs that people did...

FARMING

Every year, around the end of October, farmers dug up their fields using a wooden plow pulled by oxen. Then they sowed seeds for crops (usually barley and wheat).

Crops were harvested in March, using curved blades called sickles.

WINNOWING

Once the crops had been harvested, the grain was crushed to separate it from the husks. Then the grain was tossed into the air, so the wind blew away any last bits of husk. This is called winnowing.

Winnowers wore headscarves to stop grain husks from sticking in their hair.

MAKING WINE

To make wine, farmers crushed grapes with their feet, gripping ropes to stop themselves from slipping over. As they squished the grapes, another man collected the juice in a pot.

PICKING FRUIT

Fruit was an important part of Egyptians' diets. Most farmers grew pomegranates, figs and dates.

Hungry baboons often stole fruit from trees.

CRAFTSMEN

Skilled craftsmen, such as potters, carpenters and glassmakers, were highly respected. The tomb painting on the left shows metalworkers making necklaces and other ornaments.

Carpenters often worked together in large workshops.

BUILDERS

Some builders made houses from mud bricks. Others were involved in major royal building projects – decorating temples, or carving the kings' magnificent tombs.

SERVANTS

Wealthy houses had many servants. These hard-working people cooked their masters' food, kept their houses tidy, and served guests at their parties.

In some houses, the work was done by slaves – foreign prisoners captured in battles.

BAKING AND BREWING

This model from a tomb shows four servants preparing their master's meals...

Egyptian beer was thick and gloopy. People drank it through long straws to filter out the lumps.

About to serve a meal

Making beer from barley and bread soaked in water (the servant passes the mashed-up mixture through a sieve)

Grinding grain to make flour

Baking bread on a stove

EGYPTIANS AT HOME

Ancient Egyptians loved showing off. Rich people's homes were decorated with wall paintings, fancy furniture and beautiful pottery.

HOW THE RICH LIVED

Wealthy Egyptians lived in villas near the Nile, with up to 30 rooms, lush gardens with palm trees, and ponds for fish. The walls were painted white, to reflect the desert sun, keeping the villa cool inside.

Most ordinary Egyptians lived in small houses in towns, and did their cooking on the roof.

FURNITURE

Fine wood was very expensive, so few people owned much furniture. Most Egyptians just sat on the floor. Rich people, though, had chairs and stools, often carved with elegant lotus flowers, or lions' heads.

This chair belonged to a queen. It's carved with lotus flowers.

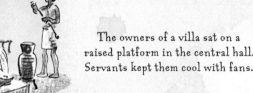

This stool is decorated with carvings of lions.

The owners of a villa sat on a raised platform in the central hall. Servants kept them cool with fans.

Egyptians tried to keep their homes neat and tidy, to reflect the natural order of the universe.

CLOTHES CHESTS

Clothes were normally stored neatly folded in wooden chests like this one on the left. People kept them in their bedrooms.

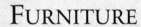

BEDS

Egyptian beds sloped down a little, from top to bottom, and had boards at the end to stop the owner from slipping off. Beds were made of wood and leather, and probably had a mattress and sheets.

Headrest at the top

HEADREST

This strange-looking object is an Egyptian pillow. At night, the owner lay with his head tucked into the curve. This headrest is carved of ivory, but most were made of wood.

This bed's legs are carved with lion paws.

POTS, PLATES AND VASES

Every Egyptian home had several pieces of pottery – plates for food, and jars for storing perfume, wine, or oil. Some were quite simple, while others were made of gold or glass, and decorated with patterns or images from nature.

These jars, made of painted glass, were used for storing cosmetics.

Most Egyptian pots were made of red clay. This jar was probably used for storing oil.

Few jars had flat bases. Instead they were kept upright on stands like these.

Shallow dishes were used by servants to serve their master his food.

ALL DRESSED UP

Although their clothes were usually quite simple, most Egyptians showed off by wearing elaborate make-up, wigs and dazzling jewels.

EGYPTIAN CLOTHES

Egyptians' clothes were usually made of thin, white linen, which kept them cool in the sweltering sun. Occasionally, people wore clothes decorated with vibrant patterns.

These statues show an Egyptian couple wearing simple linen clothes.

Some linen clothes were designed with elaborate patterns of folds.

This statue shows a servant wearing a brightly patterned dress.

COSMETICS

Both men and women wore eyeliner to help keep irritating flies away from their eyes, and perfumes to smell sweet. Women also used lipstick. Wealthy Egyptians kept these cosmetics in little pots, stored in intricately decorated boxes.

Oil and perfume jars

Brightly painted decorations

This sculpted head, of Akhenaten's wife, Nefertiti, shows the Queen wearing thick eyeliner and lipstick. She also has jewels around her neck.

Egyptians made cosmetics by mixing crushed minerals with oil. Perfumes were made from flowers and fragrant wood, crushed in oil.

JEWELS AND ORNAMENTS

Almost everyone wore some sort of ornament – necklaces, bracelets, collars or earrings. For the rich, these were made of gold and precious stones. Less wealthy people often wore necklaces made from clay beads.

To show off at parties, Egyptians wore as many accessories as they could afford.

This necklace is made of a glazed ceramic material called Egyptian faience. The pieces are painted to look like flower petals.

Some ornaments were decorated with religious symbols, to bring their owners good luck. This bracelet is decorated with the 'Eye of Horus' (you can read more about this popular Egyptian symbol on page 10).

Goldsmiths melted gold, and then shaped it into beautiful ornaments.

HAIR AND WIGS

Hair was often cut short, but rich ladies wore elaborate braided and curled wigs. This painting shows women dressed in wigs decorated with beads.

Men and women often wore cones of fat on their heads. The fat was mixed with perfume, so it left them smelling sweet as it melted.

This painting, from a tomb wall, shows women dressed for a party.

FUN AND GAMES

Egyptians enjoyed all sorts of fun activities in their spare time. Children played with toys, while adults liked board games, or watching musicians and dancers at parties.

Playing pieces

Drawer for playing pieces

SENET

Every Egyptian played board games. The most popular was 'senet', which involved moving pieces around a board. This decorated senet set probably belonged to a rich noble.

HOUNDS AND JACKALS

Hounds and jackals was a popular game, although no one today knows the rules. It involved pieces with heads shaped as hounds and jackals.

The long pieces slotted into holes on the board game's surface.

Bronze teeth

TOY ANIMALS

This wooden toy was once brightly painted, and had tiny bronze teeth. By pulling the string through the top, the owner could make the animal's mouth snap open and shut.

BALLS AND TOPS

Toy balls were usually made of leather, and stuffed with reeds. This spinning top (on the left) is made of quartz.

Spinning top

Children played 'catch' while on piggy-back.

DOLLS

This children's doll is made of linen, stuffed with rags and papyrus reeds. The face was once decorated with wool.

This decorated harp is made of wood, with strings of woven animal guts.

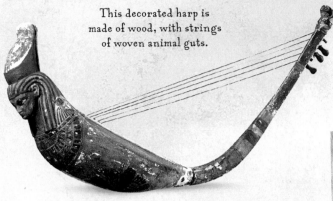

MUSICAL INSTRUMENTS

Egyptians seemed to have loved music. This tomb painting shows female musicians playing four different instruments – a harp, lute, pipes, and lyre.

Some harps were as big as their player. They rested on stands while they were played.

CLAPPERS

This instrument is made from the tusks of a hippopotamus. The two pieces were joined by twine, so that they clapped together when shaken.

Music at Egyptian festivals was full of loud claps and drums. Egyptians believed that the noises drove away evil forces.

DANCERS

As well as musicians, the best parties had professional dancers. Sometimes there were also jugglers, acrobats, singers and storytellers to keep guests entertained.

SACRED WRITING

Egyptian tombs and temple walls were covered in elaborate signs and pictures. This wasn't just decoration – it was writing. Today, we call it hieroglyphics, which means 'sacred carvings' in Greek.

HIEROGLYPHICS

Hieroglyphics was a very complex script, with over 700 signs. Some stood for letters, while others represented objects or ideas.

 This sign indicates that a word is about a god or a king.

 This hieroglyph makes the sound of the letter W.

 This hieroglyph is the letter I.

 This basket symbol represented the sound of the letter K.

 This snake hieroglyph makes the sound of DJ (or 'ju').

 This sign could mean 'house', or the sound of the letters PR.

 Some signs make the sound of two letters together. This is IR.

 This sign shows that the word before it describes an action.

 This sign is the letters ST, but it can also mean 'throne'.

 This hieroglyph is the letter N. It also means 'water'.

 This headless goat symbol means 'hide' (animal skin).

CARTOUCHES

Royal names were written inside oval frames, called cartouches. Egyptians thought the frames protected the names. These cartouches contain the official and personal names of King Horemheb.

Hieroglyphics were written by teams of artists. One drew the signs, another carved them into stone, and a third added the paint.

SCRIBES

Few Egyptians could write hieroglyphics. So, to write any important documents, they hired scribes (professional writers). Scribes were highly respected, and often became rich and powerful.

Statues of scribes usually show them sitting cross-legged, with a scroll in their laps.

Scribes studied for at least five years to learn all the complicated hieroglyphic signs.

HIERATIC

Scribes usually wrote documents, such as legal contracts or letters, in a simplified version of hieroglyphics, called hieratic. Hieratic was faster to write, but still very hard to learn.

Scribes wrote important sentences in red ink.

A SCRIBE'S TOOLS

Every scribe had their own writing palette (board), with holes for red and black ink. They mixed the ink in shells, and wrote using a brush made of a reed.

ROSETTA STONE

For centuries, no one knew how to read hieroglyphics. Then, in 1822, the mystery was solved thanks to this stone, found in Rosetta, in northern Egypt. It's carved with the same document in hieroglyphics, hieratic, and Greek. By comparing them, scholars were finally able to understand the Egyptian signs.

The meaning of hieroglyphics was solved by French scholar Jean-François Champollion.

DISCOVERING ANCIENT EGYPT

For a long time after Ancient Egyptian civilization collapsed, people didn't know much about it. Then, from the 1800s, explorers began to visit Egypt, and rediscover its glorious past.

HERODOTUS

Greek historian Herodotus is known as the 'Father of History'. He visited Egypt around 450BC, and was one of the first people to write about its past. Mostly, he wrote whatever people told him, so his facts are not always reliable.

NAPOLEON

After conquering Egypt in 1798, French military leader Napoleon Bonaparte sent 150 scholars and artists to study its monuments. Their drawings gave many people in Europe their first glimpse of Egypt's treasures.

In 1798, Napoleon's army fought Egyptian troops close to the Great Pyramid at Giza.

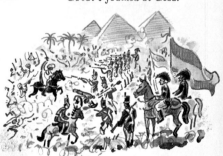

BELZONI

From 1816, Italian explorer Giovanni Belzoni toured Egypt, hunting for treasures to sell to museums. Belzoni explored temples, discovered tombs, and found the entrance to King Khafra's pyramid at Giza.

Before he became an explorer, Giovanni Belzoni worked in a circus as a strongman, known as Patagonian Sam.

Belzoni organized teams of workers to drag statues to ships on the Nile, so he could transport them to museums.

This painting shows Belzoni's workers dragging part of a colossal statue of King Ramesses II. Today, the statue head is on display in the British Museum in London.

DAVID ROBERTS

Scottish artist David Roberts toured Egypt and the Near East between 1838 and 1840. He journeyed down the Nile, sketching and painting the temples, tombs and pyramids that he saw along the way.

David Roberts and other explorers sailed up and down the Nile on sailing boats called 'dhows'.

EGYPTOMANIA

After Howard Carter discovered Tutankhamun's tomb in 1922 (see page 16), the world went Egypt-crazy. Thousands of people visited Egypt, touring tombs and ruined temples.

These tourists are taking tea at the top of the Great Pyramid. Climbing Egypt's pyramids has since been banned.

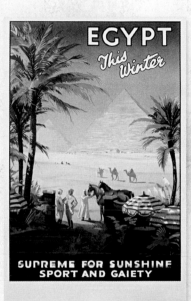

EGYPT
This Winter

SUPREME FOR SUNSHINE
SPORT AND GAIETY

FLINDERS PETRIE

British archaeologist William Flinders Petrie spent 37 years in Egypt, and found thousands of ancient objects. Unlike treasure-seekers before him, Petrie kept meticulous records of everything he found. Much of his collection is kept in the Petrie Museum, in London.

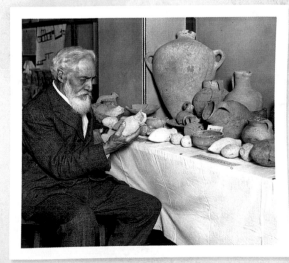

To keep cool in Egypt's hot climate, Petrie often wore only his long pink underwear as he worked.

INDEX

You can find out more about Ancient Egypt by going to the Usborne Quicklinks website at www.usborne.com/quicklinks and typing the keywords "Egypt picture book".

ACKNOWLEDGEMENTS

Cover: Howard Carter and Lord Carnarvon © Hulton-Deutsch Collection/Corbis; Inner coffin © The Metropolitan Museum of Art/Art Resource, NY/Scala Archives, ART425284; Pectoral from tomb of Tutankhamun © Photo Scala, Florence; **The Land of Egypt:** Memphis statue © DEA/G. DAGLI ORTI; Heliopolis obelisk © The Art Archive/Collection Dagli Orti; Akhenaten bust © The Art Archive/Luxor Museum, Egypt/Gianni Dagli Orti; Karnak © Ocean/Corbis; Luxor © The Art Archive/Gianni Dagli Orti; Abu Simbel © The Art Archive/Gianni Dagli Orti; Edfu © Sandro Vannini/CORBIS; Philae © Neale Clarke/Robert Harding World Imagery/Corbis; **Mighty kings:** Narmer Palette © Werner Forman Archive/Egyptian Museum, Cairo. Location: 35; Hatshepsut © Photo Scala, Florence; Mentuhotep II © The Art Archive/Egyptian Museum Cairo/Gianni Dagli Orti; Thuthmosis III © Photo Scala, Florence; Akhenaten © Greg Watts/ REX Features; Tutankhamun © Egyptian National Museum, Cairo, Egypt/The Bridgeman Art Library; Ramesses II © Photo Scala Florence/Heritage Images; Cleopatra © Photo Scala, Florence/BPK, Bildagentur fuer Kunst, Kultur und Geschichte, Berlin; **Gods and goddesses:** Great Harris Papyrus © The Trustees of the British Museum; Amun © Image copyright The Metropolitan Museum of Art/Art Resource/Scala, Florence; Book of Nedjmet © The Trustees of the British Museum; Osiris © The Trustees of the British Museum; Ma'at © Sandro Vannini/Corbis; Isis © Photo Scala, Florence; The Aten © Photo Scala, Florence; **More Egyptian gods:** Bastet © The Trustees of the British Museum; Hathor © Hemis/Alamy; Book of Nedjmet © The Trustees of the British Museum; Anubis © Robert Harding World Imagery/Corbis; Book of the Dead © The Trustees of the British Museum; Thoth ©The Art Archive/Musée du Louvre Paris/Gianni Dagli Orti; Bes © The Art Archive/Musée du Louvre Paris/Gianni Dagli Orti; **Magic charms:** Eye of Horus © The Gallery Collection/Corbis; Ankh symbol © JDDallet/ Photolibrary Group Ltd; Fish amulet © Werner Forman Archive/Royal Scottish Museum, Edinburgh. Location: 42; Heart amulet © The Trustees of the British Museum; Scarab © Sandro Vannini/Corbis; Djed pillar © age fotostock/Robert Harding; Knot of Isis © The Trustees of the British Museum; Ma'at © age fotostock/Robert Harding; **Royal tombs:** Step pyramid © So Hing-Keung/Corbis; Great Pyramid © Roger Ressmeyer/Corbis; Giza © Bildarchiv Steffens/The Bridgeman Art Library; Pyramidion © Photo Scala, Florence; Great Sphinx © Jay M. Pasachoff/Science Faction/Corbis; Valley of the Kings © The Art Archive/ Gianni Dagli Orti; Tomb © Gianni Dagli Orti/CORBIS; **Mummies and coffins:** Mummy © Thomas Hartwell/CORBIS; Gold mask © The Trustees of the British Museum; Canopic jars © The Trustees of the British Museum; Coffin of Itneb © The Trustees of the British Museum; Coffin of Nesperennub © The Trustees of the British Museum; Inner coffin © The Metropolitan Museum of Art/Art Resource, NY/Scala Archives, ART425284; Coffin stack © RMN/Les frères Chuzeville; Sarcophagus © The Trustees of the British Museum; **Royal treasures:** Howard Carter © Hulton-Deutsch Collection/CORBIS; Tutankhamun's coffin © Robert Harding World Imagery/Corbis; Funeral mask © James Strachan/Robert Harding; Ka statue © The Art Archive/Egyptian Museum Cairo/Gianni Dagli Orti; Throne © Robert Harding World Imagery/Corbis; Painted chest © Robert Harding World Imagery/Corbis; Gold box © Sandro Vannini/Corbis; Alabaster jar © Robert Harding World Imagery/Corbis; **The mighty Nile:** Fishing boats © Glow Images/Werner Forman Archive/Egyptian Museum, Cairo. Location: 40; Sailing ship © The Trustees of the British Museum; Funeral ship © The Trustees of the British Museum; Heron © The Art Archive/Bibliothèque Musée du Louvre/Gianni Dagli Orti; Geese © The Art Archive/Egyptian Museum Cairo/Gianni Dagli Orti; Fish © The Trustees of the British Museum; Hippopotamus © Kunsthistorisches Museum, Vienna, Austria/Ali Meyer/The Bridgeman Art Library; Crocodile © Heini Schneebeli/The Bridgeman Art Library; **Egyptian jobs:** Tomb painting of plowing © The Trustees of the British Museum; Winnowers © The Art Archive/Gianni Dagli Orti; Wine makers © The Art Archive/ Gianni Dagli Orti; Picking figs ©The Art Archive/Bibliothèque Musée du Louvre/Gianni Dagli Orti; Painting from tomb © The Trustees of the British Museum; Builders © The Art Archive/Gianni Dagli Orti; Cosmetic spoon © The Art Archive/Musée du Louvre Paris/Gianni Dagli Orti; Model of cooks © Gianni Dagli Orti/CORBIS; **Egyptians at home:** Book of the Dead © The Trustees of the British Museum; Chair © The Art Archive/Egyptian Museum Cairo/Gianni Dagli Orti; Stool © The Art Archive/Musée du Louvre Paris/Gianni Dagli Orti; Wooden casket © The Art Archive/Musée du Louvre Paris/Gianni Dagli Orti; Ivory headrest © Photo Scala, Florence; Egyptian bed © Werner Forman Archive/ Egyptian Museum, Cairo. Location: 41; Blue pots © Werner Forman Archive/British Museum, London. Location: 36; Embalming bottle © The Metropolitan Museum of Art/Art Resource, NY/Scala Archives ART425286; Bowl © The Trustees of the British Museum; **All dressed up:** Rahotep and wife © The Art Archive/Egyptian Museum Cairo/Collection Dagli Orti; Servant statue © Image copyright The Metropolitan Museum of Art/Art Resource/Scala, Florence; Nefertiti © Jean-Pierre Lescourret/Corbis; Make up box © Gianni Dagli Orti/CORBIS; Ear rings © Robert Harding World Imagery/Corbis; Faience necklace © The Trustees of the British Museum; Bracelet © Werner Forman Archive/Egyptian Museum Cairo (JE 72184B) Location: 42A; Banquet scene © The Trustees of the British Museum; **Fun and games:** Senet © National Geographic Image Collection/Alamy; Hounds and jackals © The Metropolitan Museum of Art/Art Resource/Scala, Florence; Doll © The Trustees of the British Museum; Toys © The Trustees of the British Museum; Harp © The Trustees of the British Museum; Musicians © The Art Archive/Bibliothèque Musée du Louvre/Gianni Dagli Orti; Clappers © The Art Archive/Musée du Louvre Paris/Gianni Dagli Orti; Wall relief © White Images/Scala, Florence; **Sacred writing:** Tomb painting © DeAgostini Picture Library/ Scala, Florence; Royal cartouches © Giraudon/The Bridgeman Art Library; Scribe © Photo Scala, Florence; Papyrus © The Trustees of the British Museum; Tablet of scribe © Photo Scala, Florence; Rosetta Stone © The Trustees of the British Museum; **Discovering Ancient Egypt:** Herodotus © Photo Scala, Florence/ BPK, Bildagentur fuer Kunst, Kultur und Geschichte, Berlin; Napoleon © The Art Archive/Diplomatic Club Cairo/Gianni Dagli Orti; Belzoni © White Images/ Scala, Florence; Belzoni workers © The Art Archive; David Roberts © The Art Archive/Bibliothèque des Arts Décoratifs Paris/Gianni Dagli Orti; Tourists on Great Pyramid © Bettmann/CORBIS; 'Egypt this winter!' © Swim Ink 2, LLC/CORBIS; Flinders Petrie © Hulton-Deutsch Collection/CORBIS

With thanks to Ruth King

Additional design by Tom Lalonde, Lucy Wain and Stephen Moncrieff
Digital manipulation by John Russell

This edition first published in 2016 by Usborne Publishing Ltd.,
Usborne House, 83-85 Saffron Hill, London, EC1N 8RT, England. www.usborne.com
Copyright © 2016, 2012 Usborne Publishing Ltd.